£4

ROYAL MARINES
DEAL

ROYAL MARINES
DEAL

A PICTORIAL HISTORY

Andrew Lane

HALSGROVE

In association with

First published in 2000 by Halsgrove
Copyright © 2000 Andrew Lane

ISBN 1 84114 081 3

British Library Cataloguing-in-Publication-Data
A CIP data for this book is available from the British Library

HALSGROVE
Halsgrove House
Lower Moor Way
Tiverton EX16 6SS
T: 01884 243242
F: 01884 243325
www.halsgrove.com

Printed and bound in Great Britain by MPG Books Ltd, Bodmin

Contents

The Coat of Arms for the Borough of Deal approved in 1968. A Royal Marine in full dress uniform stands opposite the Roman Legionary Caesius Scaeva, who was made a centurion by Julius Caesar after his Marine-like landing on Deal Beach in 55BC.

Introduction

5 54,554 recruits passed through the training Depôt at Deal, Kent. Royal Marines were made there from promising but raw material. Equally, thousands of boys, youths and more recently, young women were trained there as Royal Marines musicians and buglers. Many returned there as instructors and staff, making Deal the mother barracks of the Corps.

I trust the pedantic reader will forgive the title of this book, because it could be said that this was an official designation for only ten years. However, I wanted to cover the whole period of 1861-1996 with one short, generic title. Alternatively the more accurate title would be 'The Depôt, Royal Marines Deal (1861-1940); Royal Marines Holding Battalion, Deal (1940-43); The Depôt Royal Marines, Deal (1943-1977); Royal Marines, Deal (1977-1987); Royal Marines School of Music, Deal (1987-1996).'

The purpose of this book is to make the Deal photographs from the Royal Marines Museum, available to a wide audience. It will also be a permanent momento for an historic place and era now that the barracks have closed. Three things from my research into memoirs, records and reports stand out. Firstly how cold Deal was! Secondly despite the hard training and regime, many Royal Marines looked back on their time at Deal with respect. Finally, the affection and support of the people of Deal for the Royal Marines. For sure, the town benefited economically from the presence of the Depôt and Schools of Music, but it was more than that. There was pride and admiration of the Royal Marines in their midst.

I am grateful to the following for their assistance and support. The Director of the Royal Marines Museum, Chris Newbery; Major Alastair Donald R.M., Terry Williams, Director, Deal Maritime Museum and Captain Derek Oakley M.B.E. R.M. Joffre Swales for permission to reproduce from his book *We Blew and they were Shattered*. Basil Kidd for permission to use his photographs. Len Kerr, Capt. A. Newing R.M., H. Jimmick, Mary Pocock and Charles Bowden B.E.M. for sending in their pictures to freely use in this book. Finally a thanks to every donor of photographs to the Royal Marines Museum Library.

Andrew Lane

South Barracks were originally built for Army cavalry units in 1795. Stables and tethering rings for horses were evident when the Royal Marines used the buildings as Administrative Offices.

Before The Royal Marines

The Royal Marines were not Deal's first love. There were others in uniform before them. The Royal Navy had a thriving yard in Deal from the early seventeenth century until 1864. It was situated between the castle and the pier. The Army had been billeted in the town throughout the eighteenth century and even a barracks were built for them in Queen's Street. However, it was the titanic struggles with France from 1793 to 1815 which raised the Army's presence to a greater scale. In 1795 new larger barracks were built for infantry and cavalry. They were to be known as the North and South Barracks and were the core of the later Royal Marines Establishment.

The South Barracks, also known as Cavalry Barracks, had stables for 63 horses and accommodation for 53 men. Their first occupants were the 15th Light Dragoons. Following the conclusion of the Napoleonic War the South Barracks were partly occupied by Blockade Men who fought a different war – against smugglers (1816-1831). The Blockade Men were replaced by the Coastguards who continued the occupation until 1840.

The North Barracks were occupied by various infantry regiments until 1840. Then, along with South Barracks, they were used by a detachment of Royal Artillery. Further regiments continued the Army's presence until 1861.

One other building which was to be part of the later Royal Marines Depôt was the Royal Naval Hospital, later known as East Barracks. Before 1812 an older hospital occupied the site. It treated not only sailors but also soldiers evacuated from the Continent. When lightning struck in 1809, the old hospital was so badly damaged it was demolished and rebuilt. The new 1812 Naval Hospital, with its clock tower, was to become the most distinguishable building in Deal Barracks. The Hospital could accommodate 300 patients and its operating theatre was still there in the 1990s. Behind the Naval Hospital was a graveyard with 1685 recorded burials.

The Army's presence in Deal Barracks ended in 1869 when the Admiralty acquired the whole site in exchange for the Royal Marines Barracks of the Woolwich Division.

North Barracks with a distinctive colonnade were also built for the Army in 1795.

The Royal Naval Hospital was built in 1812 on the site of previous hospital damaged by lightning. The R.N. Hospital was re-named East Barracks in 1900.

South Barracks (1971) with the Officers' Mess looking out over lawns to Jubilee Gate.

The Royal Marines Come To Deal

Before the establishment of the Depôt in 1861, Marines had been stationed in Deal, off and on, for over two hundred years. In 1665, a year after their foundation, a party of Marines was billeted in Deal. This was during the Second Dutch War and the Marines were there to prepare a defence in case of a Dutch attack. The association continued with Marine detachments at the Royal Naval Yard until its closure in 1864.

On the barracks site, Royal Marines were billeted in the Royal Naval Hospital in 1817 probably in support of anti-smuggling operations. In 1854 Royal Marines returned to quarters in the Naval Hospital and so began a continuous presence in Deal for 142 years.

On 7 May 1861 a training Depôt was established in East Barracks. Two Officers, 16 N.C.Os and 35 Privates were drafted from the Chatham and Woolwich Divisions and their first 100 recruits arrived three days later. The first Commanding Officer was Lt Col W.R. Maxwell. The *Illustrated London News* of 24 August 1861 reported:

'The new depot barracks for recruits of the Royal Marines is now in full operation at Walmer, and a library and school have just been formed. Each married man of the establishment has a plot of land allotted to him for cultivation. The present number of inmates, chiefly recruits from the three divisions of Chatham, Portsmouth and Woolwich, is 400; and as a proof of the advantages of removing young recruits from temptations incident to garrison towns, it is worthy to remark that during the three months since the Depot has been opened no inmate has been charged before a magistrate.'

As mentioned before, when the Woolwich Division was disbanded in 1869, the North and South Barracks were acquired from the Army to create the full scale Depôt, Royal Marines, Deal. Now all recruit training for the Royal Marine Light Infantry (R.M.L.I.) was undertaken at Deal, with the Royal Marine Artillery (R.M.A.) training taking place at Eastney Barracks, Portsmouth.

The Depôt: 1870-1914

Within the three main sites of North, South and Royal Naval Hospital (East) barracks the new Depôt began to gradually grow with the necessary facilities.

At heart of recruit training was the achievement of physical fitness so the first priority was to get trained instructors. In 1871 a Superintendent of Physical Training was appointed which led to the creation of the Physical Training School at Deal. This key appointment was given to Captain J. Straghan R.M.L.I. who had been trained by the Army. The School provided physical training for recruits, trained P.T. instructors and coaches for all sports. By the early twentieth century it took six months to qualify as an Instructor, in which time they were trained in teaching skills, medical matters, P.T. theory, bayonet, sabre, boxing, swimming and vaulting. A Drill Shed and Gymnasium were built to complete the P.T. facilities.

The Swimming Bath was built in 1892 and was originally filled by tidal sea water. Swimming became a vital element in any recruit's training after a disaster in 1893 when HMS *Victoria* and HMS *Camperdown* collided off Tripoli. Sixty-eight Royal Marines were drowned mostly because they could not swim. Swimming lessons were overseen by the special appointment of a Superintendent of Swimming, the direct result of the *Victoria* disaster. The first Superintendent was, indeed, Lt Farquharson who had saved the life of Midshipman (later Admiral) Jellicoe as the *Victoria* foundered.

Recollections of swimming lessons were frequently unfavourable. Recruit W. Bishop recalled his experience in 1937:
'We were rapidly weeded out and ordered to parade at the deep end of the pool. And there we stood, shivering uncontrollably and holding our hands together to cover up the lower regions of our bodies – we were mistaken in thinking that swimming trunks would be issued. With a sardonic smile on his features, the muscle-bound physical training instructor swaggered slowly around the edge of the pool and one by one, we were pushed or shoved into the deep end. When my head bobbed up for the fourth time, I made a desperate grab for the business end of the boathook. The swimming test was quite an ordeal consisting of wearing a heavy canvas suit with capacious pockets, swimming two lengths of the pool and then staying afloat for three minutes.'

The Rifle Range on the beach below the cliffs at Kingsdown had been in existence since 1859 when a rent of 1/- (5p) per annum was recorded. By 1889 a new lease was drawn up by the Admiralty but in 1903 the land was acquired by compulsory purchase. The encroachment of the sea and erosion was a constant problem necessitating the construction of a concrete sea wall.

The main accommodation for recruits was in North Barracks but in 1900 further accommodation for 300 men was created in the converted Royal Naval Hospital, now renamed East Barracks.

A recruit's daily life in the Edwardian era began at 5.30 a.m. in summer and 6 a.m. in winter. Some were detailed for morning fatigues while the remainder cleaned the barrack room for inspection. Instruction began at 8 a.m. and lasted until 12.30 p.m. In the afternoon he worked from 2 p.m. until 4 p.m., except on Wednesday and Saturdays. The recruit attended school after parade with the opportunity for voluntary evening classes.

The recruit did more drill than his later counterparts. The most important form of drill then was extended order, based on the tactics of the day. He also spent longer at field training. Another difference a wartime or today's Marine would notice is the food. It was wholesome then but not of the same quantity or variety. At breakfast there was a jug of tea and bread with butter, syrup or marmalade. Lunch was a cooked meal but tea, the last meal of the day, consisted of tea, bread and butter. Extra money could buy supper or purchases at the Burgoo Shop by the barracks gate. Here a plate of porridge could be bought for 1d (½p), fish and chips 3½d (2p) and faggots 2d (1p). Allowances for food took a large part out of a weekly wage of 6/8d (34p).

The children of Royal Marines instructors and staff were educated in the Chapel-School building dating from 1858. Female civilian teachers taught the infants whilst the staff of the Senior School consisted of five schoolmasters and ten Royal Marines Sergeants. The schools were inspected annually by civilian Inspectors and received funds dependent on test results. This was the standard practice in schools across the country. This account of Empire Day in 1907 reflects the aspirations for children in this era;

> A large number of children of the National Schools, adjoining the Depôt Schools, were invited to witness the ceremony. The trooping of the Colours by the Depôt cadets was a very pretty start. Mr Keightley's recitation 'Our National Defences' was capitally rendered, and just the thing to instal in the hearts of the children their loyal responsibilities and their patriotic duties to their King and Empire. The children sang The 'Flag of Britain' and 'Federation' before marching back to their schools for a bun and orange.

Royal Marines Officers and others outside the Officers' Mess in 1894. Left to right (standing) Capt. E. Orlebar, Lt H. Farquharson, Lt F. Athow, Lt L.S.T. Halliday (later V.C.), Rev. J. Berry, Lt F. Edwards, Maj. C. Gordon, Maj. E. Congdon, Fleet Surgeon J. Stone, Maj. E. Innes (Sitting), Lt J. Parker, Capt. G. Byrne, Capt. & Adj. C. Trotman.

The Officers' Mess, South Barracks in 1882. The sheep make effective lawn mowers.

Jubilee Gate, South Barracks. The Officers' Mess used to have a covering of ivy over its facade.

The full compliment of the Depôt on the new Drill Ground, South Barracks 1899. The railway embankment can be seen in the background.

The Depôt fire service with their escape ladder outside South Canteen c. 1905-1912.

The Billiard Room in South Barracks c. 1890s.

The Reading Room, possibly in South Barracks but at different periods spanning the 1890s-1912. There were 5000 books in the library.

Room mates often had their photo taken as a group. These were always informal and other examples over the years appear through this book. This 1908 group also features a drummer in the centre.

The Sergeants' Mess, South Barracks c. 1910.

The Coffee Room, Sergeants' Mess, South Barracks in 1899 featuring a small stage.

DEPÔT R.M. DEAL.

Church Parade formed up in front of South Barracks c. 1910.

An interesting angle of North Barracks. In the foreground are the playground climbing frames for the Chapel School.

A 1912 scene of the Cook House with some huge roasts.

Several drill squads on the North Barracks Parade Ground. Note the targets on the left side wall. c. 1890.

Christmas in Room K2, K Block, North Barracks. Note the iron frame beds and the room's crockery/cutlery cupboard.

An overview of North Barracks, displaying its neat symmetry.

A men's room in North Barracks at a time when messing took place in the room. The straw mattresses are very evident.

North Barracks with the Adjutant's House far right.

The Chapel and Schools at the turn of the century. Later these became a concert hall and Theory Rooms for the Royal Marines School of Music.

A parade for the King's Birthday, 1912.

All recruits were taught to swim from 1893 following a tragedy at sea when many Royal Marines died needlessly because they could not swim.

An 1899 scene inside the Swimming Baths. There was tidal sea water used at this time.

The Infirmary was built in 1900 to replace the antiquated Royal Naval Hospital.

The Pharmacy c. 1904.

The Cadet Corps pose in front of the Gymnasium c. 1907.

Rope exercises in the Gymnasium c. 1905.

The Quarter Master's staff, 1896.

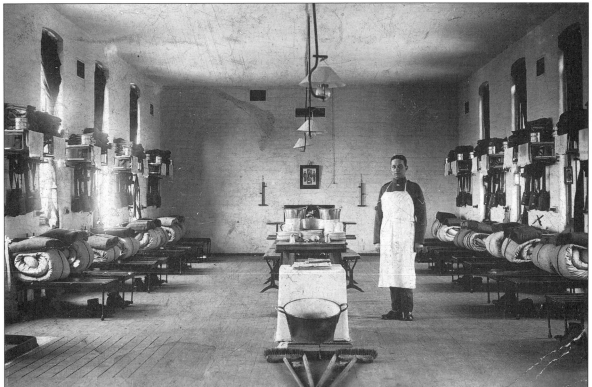

An austere barrack room prepared for the men's meal.

A novelty postcard from 1912.

Basil Kidd

The Commandant's carriage. The driver was the grandfather of Basil Kidd a Royal Marine and renowned photographer in Deal. On the wall is a bird cage containing a Mynah bird whose language was apparently quite colourful.

The front gate of the Royal Naval Hospital in 1899 just before it was renamed East Barracks.

Rowing a naval cutter was a standard part of training but this is the Commandant's Galley, built locally and of a type known as a Deal Galley, 1900.

Sports Day c. 1899-1903 in South Barracks.

The Depôt Bootmakers known as 'snobs'.

Believed to be an inspection of fitted clothing outside the Tailors' Shop

These two images of Kingsdown camps and rifle range, separated by about fifty years, shows clearly the encroachment of the sea.

The Depôt At War 1914-1918

Even before the official declaration of war with Germany in August 1914, the Depôt was on alert. Buglers sounded the 'Assembly' in the streets of Deal on 30 July 1914 and the forthcoming annual Tattoo was cancelled.

Men flocked to recruiting offices across the country and soon Deal was flooded with recruits. A new unit, the Royal Naval Division was formed at the Depôt that August. Hundreds of seamen, many from the Royal Naval Reserve, the Royal Naval Fleet Reserve and the Royal Naval Volunteer Reserve arrived to create two Naval Brigades. One Brigade moved out to Betteshanger, between Deal and Sandwich, at the beginning of September while the other Brigade was embarked at Dover on 4 October for Antwerp. A Royal Marines Brigade had been formed on 2 August made up of four Battalions, the Plymouth, Chatham, Portsmouth and R.M.A. to be concentrated at Portsmouth. Quite soon after a Deal Battalion was created to replace the R.M.A. and the Brigade relocated to Freedown, Walmer. 605 recruits were drafted to the Brigade from the Senior Squads at the Depôt who had not yet completed their training. 265 of these recruits were under eighteen years of age.

The Royal Marines Brigade had joined the other two Naval Brigades on the expedition to Antwerp. Eight days later the sailors and Royal Marines returned chastened and shocked by their experiences. The Brigades had failed to hold the port but they had delayed the German advance. On their return on 12 October 1914 each Royal Marines Battalion returned to its own Headquarters with the Deal Battalion and Brigade H.Q. remaining at the Depôt. They completed their organisation before going on to Blandford, Dorset in January 1915 and then to the terrible campaign at Gallipoli.

Another part of the Royal Naval Division, the Engineers, was also formed in the Deal area but moved into Deal to be billeted in unoccupied houses. They stayed in Deal until April 1915 before moving off to Blandford.

Recruits for the Royal Marine Light Infantry Battalions, both long and short service, received a training of only six weeks in the Depôt. During this period they were given elementary training, discipline and a grounding in Corps traditions, before leaving for Blandford where they followed the Army training course for musketry, bayoneting and bombing. It was an all too brief and inadequate training for the trench warfare of Gallipoli or the Western front. Officer training consisted of a short infantry course instead of the pre-war four year extensive programme.

Not since Napoleon had the tide of war come so close to Deal. It was inevitable therefore that there were fears of an invasion with Deal as the prime landing site. A Royal Marine Emergency Force was formed from serving ranks at the Depôt. Operation Order No 1 to this Force, dated 24 February 1916, 6 p.m., read:-

1. It is expected that a hostile landing may be attempted tonight, or in the course of the next few days.
2. The emergency force under the command of Lt Col Godfrey will man the beach trenches at night from 6.30 p.m. to one hour after reveille.
3. No. 1 Company will man the trenches from Kingsdown Coastguard Station to Walmer Castle; Old Soldiers platoon to remain in barracks.
4. No 2 Company will man the trenches thence to Deal Castle.
5. No. 3 Company will man the trenches thence to Sandown Castle.
6. One machine-gun and one crew will go with each Company – the remaining three guns will remain in Barracks.
7. Men will take one blanket each and greatcoats, and will not be in marching order, but will take filled bottles and haversacks.
8. Lt Col Godfrey's Headquarters will be Officers' Mess, South Barracks.

Immediately after this order was issued the 'Cinque Port Fencibles' were mobilised. This volunteer force of residents of the district over military age, had been formed at the start of the war. These were the Great War predecessors to the later Home Guard. On mobilisation this local defence force were issued with rifles from the Depôt with 50 rounds of ammunition. On the night of the expected invasion they remained in South Barracks Drill Shed until midnight before being sent into the trenches on the beaches. Early next morning after a snowy night, they were returned to the Depôt.

In November 1917 a new battalion was ordered to be raised with a secret mission in mind. This was to be the legendary 4th Battalion and their mission was a joint naval operation to close Zeebrugge harbour. By February 1918 the Battalion's strength was 654 with the Headquarters assembled at Deal. So overcrowded was the Depôt at this time that a portion of the Battalion was housed under the North Drill Shed, alongside some 300 men of the R.M. Labour Corps.

Training for the 4th Battalion was intense but with an objective. Outside Deal, on Freedown, attack rehearsals were made over prepared ground which was laid out in a plan of the Zeebrugge Mole. The ground was taped out and covered with strips of canvas to represent the possible features to be encountered in the attack. To improve security the rumour was put about that the Battalion was going to join the Royal Naval Division, now renamed 63rd (R.N.) Division, in France for a special raid. The training schedule also indicated the type of action the 4th Battalion could expect. In a secret memo of 10 February 1918 from the Adjutant General Royal Marines, entitled 'Suggestions as to Training', it stated:- 'The object of the training is to get the men physically fit, full of dash and accustomed to short sharp raids by night, equipped in the highest order.' Heavy marching was not required, nor digging or open warfare tactics. Instead they should be proficient in trench fighting, grenade throwing and night work.

The training schedule was halted for two V.I.P. visits. On 2 March 1918 the Battalion was inspected by the Adjutant General Royal Marines Sir David Mercer followed on the 7 March by King George V. The training resumed for a further month before the Battalion entrained at Deal for Dover on 6 April.

In the attack on Zeebrugge the 4th Battalion was badly mauled. However the courage of the Royal Marines on that day became one of the great moments in the history of the Corps. Fifty per cent of the 4th Battalion were killed or wounded. The survivors marched back into Deal Barracks at 10.30 a.m. the next morning. There were no counsellors waiting to help with trauma the men must have been experiencing but they had strength of comradeship. Then came the announcement that the King would award two Victoria Crosses by the Ninth Statute of the decoration, that is, a force commander is unable to single out an individual for gallantry, but there was collective gallantry. A secret ballot was held at Deal on 26 April to select one Officer and one Other Ranks to receive Victoria Crosses. The ballot winners were Capt. E. Bamford D.S.O., R.M.L.I. and Sgt N.A. Finch, R.M.A. On 27 April the 4th Battalion was dispersed and a 4th Battalion has never been formed again in recognition of the gallantry at Zeebrugge.

Returning to the visit by the King on 7 March 1918, this was an occasion of more than the usual significance. This took the usual form of displays by numerous squads. The King met a Private Ingle, a recruit, who had joined in December 1914 at the age of thirteen years and eleven months and served for two years with the R.M. Brigade in Gallipoli and France, where he was wounded in July 1916. Subsequently discharged 'mis-statement as to age', he re-enlisted in January 1918 aged sixteen years ten months.

It was when the King was in the Officers' Mess that the suggestion was made that the Senior Squad of the long service recruits should be called 'King's Squad'. This in turn led to the best all round Senior Squad recruit becoming a King's Badge man.

When the Armistice that ended the First World War was announced on 11 November 1918, the Adjutant of the Depôt went in to see the Commandant at 10 a.m. to say something ought to be done to celebrate the occasion. The Commandant, Brigadier General C. Parsons said, 'Is it really necessary?'

However the whole Depôt was paraded on South Green at noon for a short church service and the Commandant's address. His address was very brief and he ended by saying, 'The remainder of the day will be a holiday and tomorrow we will start training for the next war.'

New recruits, possibly destined for the Western Front in the First World War. Two months after the start of the Battle of the Somme this group must have wondered what lay ahead for them.

In every group of new recruits there was an old soldier in charge of their room. Did they follow his advice and guidance?

King George V with the Depôt officers during his visit in March 1918. Among this group were the officers of the 4th Battalion soon to see action at Zeebrugge.

12th Platoon, 4th Battalion Royal Marines. Not an inspiring looking group but they were to show exemplary courage during the attack on Zeebrugge.

HMS Vindictive in Dover Harbour showing all the scars of the vicious fighting that took place at Zeebrugge.

The remnants of the 4th Battalion marched back into barracks after the Zeebrugge raid.

Peace Day 1918 at the Depôt. A day of celebration even if that did mean that the rare creature, the Royal Marines Piper, was allowed to play.

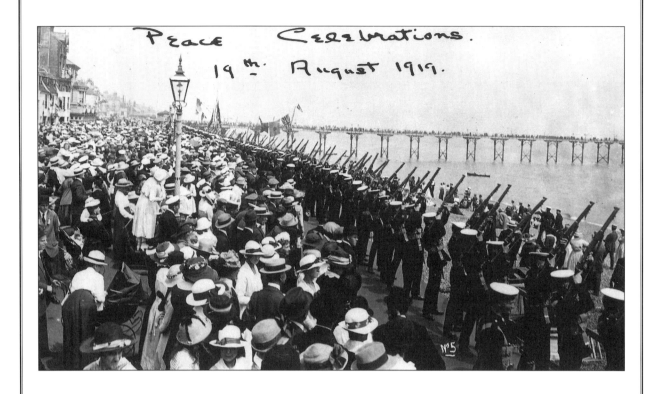

The war may have ended on 11 November 1918, but peace was not officially declared until August 1919. The townspeople of Deal and the Royal Marines of the Depôt join together to celebrate the end of 'the War to end all wars'.

The Depôt: The Inter War Years

In 1919 the Depôt returned to the routine of peace time training. Very little changed from the Edwardian era. Discipline was hard and the living conditions were basic. The training period in the 1920s was long at fifty two weeks and not considered particularly time-efficient. During the 1930s the basic training was reduced to thirty weeks. In contrast the number of recruits was low in the 1920s – only 175 enlisted in 1928. However by 1937 there were 1000 enlistments.

The life of a Royal Marines' recruit at the 1920s Depôt began as usual at Deal Station. A Barrack Room had 20 beds, each with a straw filled mattress covered with a white blanket and maybe a brown rug. The iron fireplace had the imprint of Queen Victoria's coat of arms. The immense cast iron coal bunker sat alongside and one recruit recalls it being painted perfectly white and empty of coal. There was a large trestle table whose top was bleached white by constant scrubbing with caustic soda. The walls were a sort of a beige colour and the windows were opened to the regulation 12.5 inches top and bottom. Above each bed were shelves to contain five pairs of trousers and five tunics (two Blues, two Khaki Drills, one Khaki Service Dress), a white helmet in its cover and a steel helmet.

The recruits' first days involved being kitted out, two days on Corps history and a bit of drill out of the sight of everyone else. They were taught how to stand, breathe and every aspect of marching. There could be no leave for three months but they were now earning 18/- (80p) a week. If there were any regrets about joining then the price for purchasing discharge was £50.

In addition to the daily routine of keeping the room clean, polishing buttons, blancoing belts, inspections, parades, the training syllabus lasted eight to twelve months. There was shooting, bayonet training, physical training, sports, swimming and boat pulling in a naval cutter.

The increased number of recruits in the mid-1930s prompted some expansion at the Depôt. In 1937 the Officers' Mess was extended with wings either side. In 1934 two rooms in the Mess were cabins bookable for 1/6d (8p) per night for a maximum of three consecutive nights. It cost an extra 1/- (5p) if a coal fire was required. Other facilities in the Mess were a library, billiard room and card room.

In 1937 the Admiralty bought 30 acres of farm land to be converted into playing fields. Known as Coldblow, after the farm, the playing fields were half an hour's walk from South Barracks and provided cricket, hockey and rugby fields. A new pavilion was built with a kitchen, baths, changing rooms, eating area and balcony. Another sport facility in the Depôt was the new gymnasium built in 1939 with a capacity to seat 3000 in the event of a boxing match or to be divided into two smaller gyms. Additionally there was a new changing room and a lecture room.

The Duke of York visits the Depôt 1928. Lt Col F. Griffiths escorts the Duke from the Church.

During his visit the Duke of York is enlightened about the pace stick by the Adjutant Capt. Chater.

When peace time recruit training resumed the course could be as long as a year. The inmates of room E10 do not seem overly happy about their situation.

A squad on Deal beach during knot tying instruction 1921.

The wedding of an unidentified officer surrounded by his S.N.C.Os c.1925.

The officer groom and his new wife are traditionally pulled out of South Barracks. c.1925.

One of the men's rooms in North Barracks 1929.

Church Parade c.1930 but why the men are in khaki drill is a mystery.

A group of officers c.1930.

Officers and their chargers c.1936 outside the Officers' Mess.

F. G. SMITH,

Wholesale & Retail Tobacconist,

52 HIGH STREET,
DEAL.

MESSES SPECIALLY CATERED FOR.

The Adjutant's staff, October 1937.
(Back) Cpl Gibson, Cpl Muldowney, Sgt Burden, Sgt Windle, Cpl Buscall, Sgt Ghagan, Sgt Fishlock, Cpl Packwood, Cpl Carter.
(Centre) C.Sgt Lord, Sgt Fahey, C.Sgt Kerley, C.Sgt Chadwick, Sgt Butcher, C.Sgt Brannan, Sgt Taylor, C/Sgt Smith, Sgt Fuller,
C.Sgt Avey.   (Front) Q.M.S.I. Fletcher, Q.M.S.I. Barnett, Sgt Maj. Ferneyhough, Capt.R. Simmonds (Adjutant),
Brig. R. Lough (Commandant), S/Sgt Major Sparkes, Q.M.S.I. Chivers. Q.M.S.I. Hurley.

264 and 265 Squads on The King's Birthday 1937.

H.R.H. The Prince of Wales inspecting the Guard of Honour during his visit in 1935.

The rare privilege of the King's Badge being presented by the Prince of Wales. The recipient is Recruit A.J. Payton 212 Squad.

Cricket nets in East Barracks, summer 1939.

Band Boys and Musicians on South Barracks Drill Field, summer 1939.

The Depôt: The Second World War

If the inhabitants and Royal Marines at Deal felt that the Great War came too close for comfort, the Blitzkrieg of 1940 brought the Front right up to Deal. As the number of recruits escalated dramatically, there was, first the Phoney War era of September 1939 to April 1940, then Dunkirk and the imminent threat of invasion. Like Julius Caesar and Napoleon, Hitler also knew the prime landing area was at Deal. The Depôt recruits and young officers manned positions on Deal seafront and on the golf course. Steamrollers were commandeered as road blocks.

In August and September 1940 the Battle of Britain raged above Kent and Sussex. Recruits and 'old sweats' equally stared up at the deadly aerial combat above them. Then on 7 September at 16.15 hours the Observer Posts at Deal saw the largest attack force ever seen until then, flying above them. 348 bombers and 617 fighters of the Luftwaffe were on their way to the first major bombing of London. The Blitz had begun. On 11 September Deal and Dover were bombed and shelled from huge guns in France.

Deal from henceforth suffered from shelling and 'hit and run' bombing attacks. On 4 October 1940 eight civilians were killed in Middle Street and Union Street. In December two farm workers from Deal were awarded the George Medal for continuing to work in the cliff-top fields despite being frequently straffed by aircraft and shelled from France. 1942 however saw the first period of serious attacks. 6 May, seven killed and ten homes destroyed. Two days later three more were killed in the town. 18 May, two killed; 11 August eight killed and six seriously hurt following straffing and bombing. 22 October 15 killed and seven seriously injured by bombing. Finally the most tragic single loss was the shelling of Deal on 20 January 1944 when ten were killed in their shelters, two were killed in the street and 17 were seriously injured.

In the Depôt the constant air raid threat was seriously disrupting training. There was real danger too. In one bombing raid three officers and some other ranks were killed near the Officers' Mess. The Messroom windows were blown in but no structural damage was sustained. The Depôt was becoming too much of a hot spot for mass recruit training, so all ranks training and the R.N. School of Music were evacuated. Many of the elements that made up the Depôt moved to the R.M. Reserve Depôt, Exton (today it is the Commando Training Centre, Lympstone), which became the R.M. Depôt. Regular recruit training was undertaken at the Divisions. The School of Music also moved to the West Country, before ending up for the duration of the war with the Boys in the Isle of Man and the Seniors at Scarborough.

The Depôt at Deal was re-designated the Royal Marines Holding Battalion, Deal. However the demand for Royal Marines meant that training gradually began to return to Deal. By the end of 1942 there were 2000 ranks, mainly Hostilities Only (H.O.) squads, in the barracks and at Kingsdown. In early 1943 the Royal Marines Holding Battalion status was dropped and reverted to the Depôt, Royal Marines, Deal.

Meanwhile the area around Deal was bristling with military activity. Nearby, at St Margaret's Bay, the Royal Marine Siege Regiment manned two huge 14in cross-Channel guns known as Winnie and Pooh. Royal Marines also manned the coast defence guns in Deal Castle. Kingsdown Holiday Camp was taken over and became the Weapon and Tactical Training Camp. Captain David Powell R.M. was the Tactical Training Officer and he recalls the austerity of the camp compared to the facilities at the Depôt. Night exercises were a key part of the training at Kingsdown.

The School for N.C.O.s was formed at Deal in 1940 to provide a six week course for aspiring leaders. Part of the gymnasium in the South Drill Shed was set aside as a classroom where a varied syllabus was followed. Daily instruction included Bren gun handling and stripping, instruction of recruits in rifle, bayonet and grenade, field training, tactical employment of weapons, street and village fighting, map reading and sketching. Finally, each candidate had to give a short lecture. The instructors used a variety of teaching aids including sand-table demonstrations and a magnetic blackboard.

A completely new breed of fighting man appeared at Deal in 1942 – Royal Marines Commandos. The signal had gone out calling for Royal Marines volunteers for hazardous duties. On 14 February 1942 the first aspiring commandos began to assemble at North Barracks. Initially known as 'The Royal Marine Commando', then briefly for one week 'A' Royal Marine Commando, it was finally designated 40 Royal Marine Commando with its Commanding Officer Lt Col J.Picton Phillipps.

The volunteers for selection were put through a series of vigorous medicals and tests. Many did not pass the demanding standard, but for those chosen there was a training programme unlike any they had experienced before. As commandos they trained in close quarter fighting, weapons, swimming, P.T. and 20-mile marches. The bombed-out buildings in Deal were used for street fighting exercises. All this training took place in a matter of weeks and on 5 April, with the Commando strength at 446, they moved to Scotland.

48 Royal Marine Commando was also formed at Deal but their stay was brief. Between 2 and 13 March 1944 the 7th Battalion arrived, were re-designated 48 R.M. Commando, and moved on to Achnacarry, Scotland for three weeks training. On 6 June 1944 '48' landed in Normandy on D-Day, only three months after being formed at Deal.

Several new Royal Marines units were formed at Deal during the war. Some were straightforward infantry units like the 31st, 32nd and 33rd Royal Marine Battalions in January 1945. Others were technical like the Royal Marine Engineers whose officers were civil engineers and the men came from trades. There were also specialist units like the Royal Marine Boom Defence Scaffolding Unit who were formed in December 1942. They built sea-fire coast defences which cast fire on the sea's surface in the face of an invasion.

The Royal Marine Siege Regiment manned two Cross Channel 14 inch guns at St Margaret's Bay.
This one was known as 'Winnie'.

Several new units were formed at the Depôt during the war. This Royal Marine Engineers Squad became Detachment 470. Other formations were 40 and 47 Royal Marine Commando.

The Depôt: 1945-1977

On 14 February 1945 the Borough of Deal conferred the great tribute of the Honorary Freedom of Deal on the Royal Marines. This was the first occasion such an honour had been given to the Royal Navy or Royal Marines.

The late 1940s and 1950s was a period of radical changes and uncertainty for the Royal Marines. From a wartime strength of 74,000 the Corps was down to 13,000 in 1948 with only 2000 serving at sea. Questions were asked on the need and viability of the Royal Marines in a new age of a declining sea service. The Harwood Committee reviewing the armed services and imposing cuts proposed that the Royal Marines should be disbanded. The crisis was averted by the agreed scaling down of numbers and the closure of Chatham Barracks. By 1959 the total strength was about 9000 with only a dozen detachments at sea.

With the future of the Corps saved for the moment a new era of modernisation began at the Depôt. The Admiralty planned for a Depôt training 1000 adult recruits, there were now National Servicemen as well as regulars, and the Leethart Architect Company was commissioned to re-develop the site. However the Leethart plan was never fully completed due to cut backs in defence spending and further reductions in the Corps. A new intake block in Canada Road was completed in 1950, the Dining Hall and North Barracks Naafi in 1951 and the North Barracks Drill Shed shortly afterwards. The peak of the development came in 1956 with a thoroughly modern Accommodation Block, luxurious in comparison with other Royal Marines barracks accommodation. Finally three old Victorian blocks in North Barracks were modernised but plans for re-shaping the Officers' Mess never materialised.

The winds of change were not confined to bricks and mortar. The organisation was changing too. The N.C.O. School moved away to Bickleigh, at the end of 1946. The amalgamation in 1950 of the Divisional Bands with the Royal Naval School of Music, renamed the Royal Marines School of Music, centralised musical training at Deal. The Physical Training School, responsible for the training and re-qualification of the 130 Physical Training Instructors in the Corps, serving ashore and afloat in Royal Navy and Royal Marines Establishments and ships, was re-styled the Physical Training Wing in 1957.

Youth entry was introduced in 1958 to allow in those aged sixteen to seventeen years to join as Junior Marines. Basic training comprised of fifty-two weeks at Deal, Infantry for ten weeks, Commando training of six weeks at Lympstone, seamanship training two weeks and a final two weeks at Eastney. This was the same as the adult recruit's training except that they spent fifteen weeks at Deal.

In 1960 this era of rapid change concluded with the return of the W.R.N.S. to Deal. Even the standard infantry weapon changed. The S.L.R. replaced the No 4 rifle introduced in 1939. In 1960 the Depôt was getting a steady intake of 650 regulars a year. The Junior Wing was 300 strong with Junior Musicians, Buglers and Marines. The following year, 1961, the Depôt celebrated its centenary.

A decade of stability ended in April 1969 with a reorganisation at the Depôt. The old Recruit and Junior Wings were abolished and they were replaced by a new-look Commando Wing and Music Wing. The Commando Wing undertook Adult Recruitment and Junior Marine training. The Adult squads did seven weeks in the wing before moving to the Infantry Training Centre Royal Marines (I.T.C.R.M.), Lympstone. The Juniors did thirteen weeks before joining the Adult squad on their sixth week. In 1972 all Adult training moved to the Commando Training Centre Royal Marines (C.T.C.R.M.), Lympstone.

The Music Wing undertook training of all Junior Musicians and Buglers. The training period was reduced from thirty-four weeks to twelve weeks.

So by the mid-1970s the Depôt had lost its role for Adult Recruit training but retained Junior entries and the Royal Marines School of Music. The Junior Recruit undertook a thirteen week course at Deal learning about fieldcraft, map reading, weapon training, elementary night work, swimming lessons and an intensive course of Swedish Physical Training. Juniors then left for a further fourteen weeks at C.T.C. By 1976 the Depôt was dealing with only a fraction of its capacity. There were five Junior Marine Troops under training in the Commando Wing and 100 Junior Musicians and Buglers in the Music Wing.

1977 was a dramatic year in the history of the Royal Marines in Deal. The future of the Depôt was now in real question and there were proposals for its closure. The people of Deal made their feelings well known, with a campaign called 'Keep the Marines in Deal' which ended with a petition to the Navy Minister. The Under-Secretary of State for Defence for the Royal Navy, Mr Patrick Duffy, M.P., made a visit to the Depôt in March 1977. There followed an announcement that gave the Depôt an extended lease of life. 41 Commando R.M. was to re-form on 19 July 1977 and they were to be based at the Depôt. Consequently the Depôt was to be re-named Royal Marines, Deal on 1 October 1977. The Royal Marines School of Music's permanent location was still undecided but meanwhile it was to remain at Deal. Finally, all Junior Recruit training would be moved to C.T.C.R.M. from September 1977 with the Physical Training Wing moving to C.T.C. in 1978.

30 September 1977 was to be the great day of change. 229 Troop were the last to complete their initial training at Deal. The Depôt then ceased to exist having trained 554,554 recruits in its 116 year history. Colonel David Shallow, M.C., R.M., Commanding Officer of the Depôt and Commandant of the R.M. School of Music handed over command to Lt Col Tom Seccombe, Commanding Officer of 41 Commando R.M. Major Roger Brind became Commanding Officer of the Base Organisation as Barrack Commandant. Lt Col Paul Neville O.B.E., M.V.O., F.R.A.M., Principal Director Music, also became the Commandant of the Royal Marines School of Music.

In February 1945 the Royal Marines received the honour of the Freedom of Deal.

The Freedom cemented the close relationship between the town and the Royal Marines.

General Hunton received the casket containing the Freedom of Deal Scroll.

Vice Admiral Earl Mountbatten visiting the Depôt in 1950. Col P.Smith-Hill, C.O. The Depôt is in attendance with Sgt G. Gray (left).

Winston Churchill inspecting a Guard of Honour on the day when the great man received the Freedom of Deal. 1951.

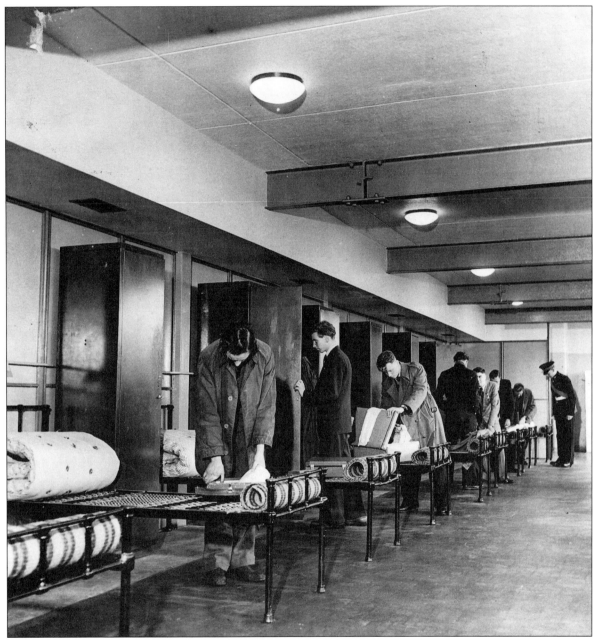

The Recruits' first day. The scene is inside the new Intake Block, North Barracks. 1950.

A very early attempt at marching. A certain Monty Python sketch comes to mind.

The Sergeant Tailor ensuring that the regulation 14 inches from the ground is achieved on this greatcoat.

Log exercises on the Drill Field.

Recruit Squads at Arms Drill in South Barracks in 1952, rehearsing for a Tattoo.

A King's Squad at Arms Drill in the Drill Shed c.1958.

A King's Squad ready for Passing Out.

Cpl W. F. Bond,   Cpl C. Fulton,   Cpl T. W. Carr,   Sgt M. H. Ford,   C/Sgt P. Bly,
Cpl A. J. Sayers,   C/Sgt W. H. Hoskins,   Sgt A. Laming,   Cpl J. T. Capner,   Cpl M. Freeborn,   Sgt R. Kingshott
C/Sgt J. Edwards,   Cpl P. W. Lewis,   Cpl T. I. Bevan,   Sgt G. King,   Sgt A. Walton,   Cpl W. J. Bryan,   Sgt T. Jenkins
Q.M.S. C. U. McLennan,   Jack Lacey,   Capt. W.B. Mansell, M.C., R.M.,   Q.M.S. F. J. Yardley   Q.M.S. W. Thomas
(First Drill)   (Regimental Sgt. Major)   (Adjutant)   (First Drill)   (First Drill)

K Block ready for inspection.

The Dining Hall, North Barracks, c.1954.

The Parade for the visit of H.M. Queen Elizabeth, The Queen Mother on 23 May 1956 to open the New Accommodation Block in North Barracks.

The Commissioning Service for the new accommodation block conducted by the Rev. F. Pocock in the presence of H.M. Queen Elizabeth, The Queen Mother and Col Lumsden, 23 May 1956.

Presentations to H.M. Queen Elizabeth, The Queen Mother during her visit on 23 May 1956. From left; Lt Col V. Dunn, Mrs Dunn (hidden), Rev. F. Pocock, Mrs Mary Pocock, Surg. Commander Burden, Mrs Burden.

The 1960 Tattoo. Traditionally held in South Barracks but on this occasion it was in North Barracks.

The scale of the Tattoo was huge and extremely well produced. This shows the clearing-up operation, 1960.

A Drumhead service conducted by Rev. F. Pocock for squads at Sandwich Camp June 1955. O.C. Capt. Dickie Meadows on far right.

The Depôt Royal Marines Ladies Rifle Club. 1960. Back row: Mrs Shillitto, Mrs Kauffman, Mrs Powell, Q.M.S. Scott, Mrs Haigh. Front row: Mrs Bach Mrs Thomas Mrs Houghton Mrs Youngson Mrs Pound.

The Centenary of the Depôt in 1961 was celebrated with a series of concerts and civic events.

The Centenary Parade with the Senior Squad drill display.

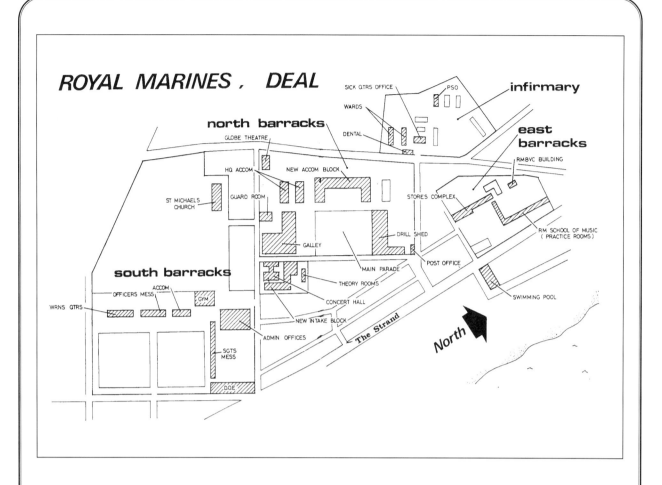

ROYAL MARINES , DEAL

SICK QTRS OFFICE
PSO
infirmary
WARDS
DENTAL
north barracks
GLOBE THEATRE
east barracks
HQ ACCOM
NEW ACCOM BLOCK
RMBVC BUILDING
ST MICHAELS CHURCH
GUARD ROOM
STORES COMPLEX
RM SCHOOL OF MUSIC (PRACTICE ROOMS)
GALLEY
DRILL SHED
MAIN PARADE
POST OFFICE
south barracks
THEORY ROOMS
OFFICERS MESS
ACCOM
GYM
CONCERT HALL
SWIMMING POOL
WRNS QTRS
NEW INTAKE BLOCK
ADMIN OFFICES
The Strand
North
SGTS MESS
DOE

The Centenary gates, North Barracks, were presented to the Depôt by the Mayor, Cllr K. Hopkinson.

Basil Kidd

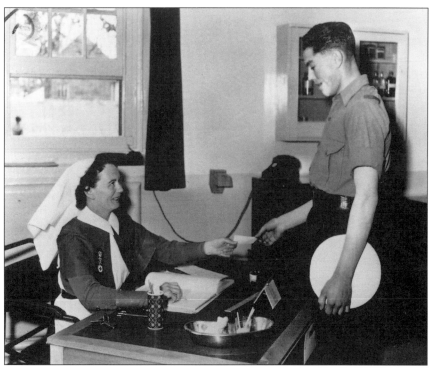

A Q.A.R.N.N.S. Sister in the Junior Wing of the Royal Marines School of Music.

Self service catering for Recruits, North Barracks, c.1966.

Basil Kidd

Col R. Houghton, the departing Commanding Officer, leaving the Depôt in the traditional manner.

The Adjutant, Capt. Mansell explains some point to the Captain General, H.R.H. Prince Philip during a visit in 1957. Also in the escorting party are R.S.M. Jack Lacey, General Campbell Hardy and Col Lumsden.

H.R.H. Prince Philip inspecting the Guard of Honour at the opening of the new Deal Pier, January 1958.

A charger with groom at the Depôt. The riding boot is reversed in the stirrups for an unknown funeral in the 1960s.

New recruits arrive at Deal station c.1967.

Weapon training with the S.L.R., 1961.

87 Troop marching past Deal Castle with Capt. Newing leading, 1974.

Remembrance Day Parade 1973.

Junior Marines in the 1970s. Junior training was transferred to Lympstone, Devon in September 1977 and 'Depôt' was dropped from the title of the unit.

41 Commando Royal Marines

The formation of 41 Commando R.M. at Deal 1977 threw the barracks into a frenzy of activity and modification. The needs and facilities for a Commando unit were quite different to a Depôt and School of Music. To make matters worse the newly formed unit was tasked to deploy to Northern Ireland in February 1978 only six months away.

Drafts poured into Deal from other Royal Marines units to bring 41 Commando up to a strength of 600. However a third rifle company was still absent. Salerno Company, the only surviving part of the previous 41 Commando, was based in Malta and they were not due to return until early 1979.

A complete scale of equipment and vehicles was arriving at Deal, including the additional stores required for a Northern Ireland tour. A new custom-built store and armoury were built but accommodation was limited. The Officers' and Sergeants' Messes were bulging but new living accommodation in the Sergeants' Mess was created in early 1978. Married quarters were in short supply so some Army quarters in Canterbury, Folkestone and Shorncliffe were taken up.

The training areas were not as suitable as those in the West Country. However places like Ashdown Forest, R.A.F. Manston were used including the Lydd/Hythe training area for all pre-Northern Ireland deployments.

The relationship between the Commando and its fellow occupants of Royal Marines, Deal was also a novelty. The Command Structure meant that 41 Commando R.M. came under Commando Forces, Plymouth; the Royal Marines Deal Base Organisation came under Training Group, Portsmouth as did the Royal Marines School of Music. The W.R.N.S. detachment were part of the Base Organisation or R.M. School of Music unless of course they were lent to 41 Commando and therefore under Commando forces. There were three separate Registries, two Motor Transport sections, a shared signal centre, two medical sections in a shared sick bay, two Provost sections, two stores organisations, one galley and two sets of standing orders. The R.S.M. had an unusual range of responsibilities. He was from 41 Commando, but as Senior Warrant Officer at Royal Marines, Deal he was responsible to the C.O. 41 Commando (Commando Forces), the Barracks Commandant (Training Group) and the Commandant R.M. School of Music (Training Group) for all S.N.C.Os at Deal.

41 had an active, if short, life. There were deployments to Northern Ireland (1978 and 1980), Cyprus (1979) and Ceremonial London Duties (November 1978). Sadly the Commando was disbanded on 20 May 1981 and three ceremonies were organised to mark the event. On 14 May the Commando made their farewell march through Deal and excercising their right as freemen to march with 'bayonets fixed, drums beating and Colours flying'. The final disbandment parade was on 20 May, when 41 Commando trooped the Colour before the Captain General, H.R.H. the Prince Philip. Finally at a Drumhead Service at Stonehouse Barracks, Plymouth the Colours were laid up in the Officers' Mess.

Maj. Gen. Pringle meets some men of Echo Company, 41 Commando 1979. '41' had reformed at Deal in 1977.

Commandos at the Kingsdown Range late 1970s.

Earl Mountbatten, a Colonel Commandant Royal Marines, with the Officers of the Guard for the forthcoming London duties.
November 1978. Back row: Lt Keogh, Lt Bell, 2/Lt Stewart, Capt. Ward, 2/Lt Taylor, Lt Appleby, Lt Hollington.
Front row: Capt. Keeling, Maj. Mason, Earl Mountbatten, Lt Col Seccombe, Capt. Pennefather.

Earl Mountbatten in the Sergeant's Mess of 41 Commando and enjoying a welcome from the P.M.C.
Vic Sylvester and the R.S.M.

The assault course for 41 Commando in South Barracks Drill Field.

Trooping the Colour, 41 Commando in North Barracks 20 May 1981. East Barracks in the background.

Trooping the Colour, 41 Commando. Only the Royal Marines School of Music kept the R.M. presence in Deal after this parade when 41 Commando was disbanded.

The Church

The first church in the Barracks was built in 1858. This was the 'Chapel-School' so called because of its dual purpose of being a school on weekdays and a Sunday place of worship.

However, a more single-purpose church capable of holding 1000 worshippers was planned for. In 1905 the foundation stone for a new church was laid by Lord George Hamilton, Captain of Deal Castle and a former First Lord of the Admiralty. A casket containing coins, a copy of *The Times* and a record of the event was sealed in the stonework.

The Church of St Michael and All Angels was of the same design as Eastney and Chatham. The church was consecrated in January 1907.

The Church of St Michael and All Angels was the first church built for the Royal Marine Light Infantry and it was described at the time as 'The Mother Church of the Red Marines'. A committee was formed to plan the design of the stained glass windows and a Mr C. Kempe, a renowned artist in stained glass for cathedrals, was employed. The cost for each window was £25 and their subject matter concentrated on Jesus, armed angels, warrior saints and apostles.

Of all the many memorials to be erected over the years, the most ironically poignant must be the two to Royal Marines killed by Irish Republican terrorists. Yet there is a gap of sixty-six years between the two memorials. In 1923 a Memorial Table was unveiled and dedicated to those who gave their lives whilst serving with the 8th Battalion, Royal Marines in Ireland from 1919-1922. The second memorial was to the 11 bandsmen killed by the I.R.A. at Deal on 22 September, 1989.

A strong moral crusade of the Victorian era was to get men to give up alcohol and to sign a pledge of abstention. Hard drinking was prevalent and several diary accounts refer to this. However the following table by the Royal Navy Temperance Society in 1903 records the alleged success at the Depôt, Royal Marines, Deal.

Pledges Taken

1885	162	1891	789	1897	1069
1886	293	1892	957	1898	993
1887	336	1893	1232	1899	653
1888	356	1894	905	1900	810
1889	1190	1895	600	1901	1274
1890	870	1896	1017	1902	905
				Total	14,411

G. Coan
Scripture Reader

The Depôt Church of St Michael and All Angels was consecrated in 1907. It replaced the small Chapel and School.

The nave was the home to the old Woolwich Division Colours.

The altar of St Michael and All Angels.

A stained glass window dedicated to the memory of Lt Col C. Congdon R.M.

A side altar at St Michael's.

The Concert Band play to a capacity audience during the last years of the R.M.S.M.

Sport

Sports Day September 1918. The high jump winner achieved 5ft 9in.

1918 Sports Day. A bizarre event for W.R.N.S. called Musical Chairs on Bicycles.

Apparently the object of this event was for the man in the barrow to put a long pole cleanly through the hole. If he misses and hits the bucket then the bucket's contents would come raining down.
Sports Day 1918.

Obstacle Race for four-man teams. A bit tough on the last man to get over unaided.

Gen. Campbell Hardy presenting the Young Soldiers Trophy to Marine Chittell, Corps Boxing Championships, Depôt R.M. 1960.

41 Commando Boxing 1981.

A line out, 1960s.

Basil Kidd

A short corner is taken on the South Barracks hockey field. 1958.

Gymnastics display team 1899.

Epée training, c.1960.

Members of 221 and 222 Troops training for the National Tug of War Championships coached by C.Sgt Havenhand and Cpl Hannah. 1976.

The water polo team c.1969. Lt R. Helme and C. Sgt. W. Bell with Gloucester House, Junior Wing, R.M.S.M.

A hunt leaves from the Officer's Mess c.1935. Brig. H. Blount and Lt Col I. Dewhurst (on the grey) and Lt Col H. Newman with members of the West Street Hunt.

*The Depôt had a well earned reputation for outstanding cricket teams. This team is from an unknown date but it must be after April 1918. Back Row: Pte. J.G. Williams, Capt Eagles Capt Spooner, Sergt R. Hill,   Sergt J. Russell.
Front Row: Revd Jones, Capt Herford, Major Little, D.C. Robinson, Capt Hall.*

The Royal Marines, Deal, winners of the 1950 Mead Cup. Ligertwood took 6 for 24.
Back row – Lt Sivil, Cpl Ridge, Q.M.S. Day, Q.M.S. Catchpole, Lt Perkins, Maj. Terry, M. Goodchild.
Centre row – B/M Jemmett, Lt Marsden, Col Smith-Hill, Instr. Lt Aynsley, Q.M.S. Ligertwood.
Front row – Surg. Comd. Benson, Musn Gardiner.

Four runs?

Cadets

A Royal Marine Cadet Corps, Deal, 1908. The Cadets Corps at Deal was formed in 1903.

1915 was an outstanding year for the Cadets and established their reputation as world-class shootists. In 1915 they won the King's Shield (National Cadets competition) and The Imperial Challenge Shield for Seniors and Juniors (British Empire Cadets competition). The Cadets went on to win the Imperial Challenge Shield repeatedly in the 1920s until they were not allowed to keep the award and instead it was presented to the unit that came second.

Maj. Keeling inspecting the R.M. Cadets at Deal, December 1978

The Globe Theatre

The Globe Theatre in the early 1900s.

A scene from HMS Misfire *in the Globe, 1894.*

The programme cover for the same production.

The cast of HMS Pinafore *by Gilbert and Sullivan .*

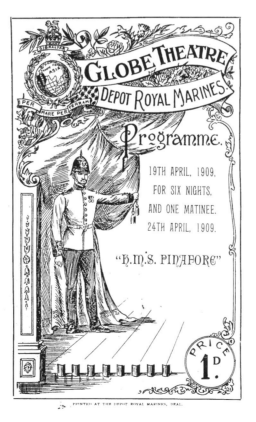

....and its programme.

The infamous Sergeants' Pantomime 1960.

It's 1988, the Sergeants' Pantomime, Corps de Ballet, and it is still outrageous.

W.R.N.S.

The W.R.N.S. was formed in 1917 and this 1918 group at the Depôt illustrates the first uniform.

W.R.N.S. returned to Deal in 1939 and were billeted in the hotel 'Fair Maid of Kent' on Canada Road. This is the Victory Parade in Deal 1945.

Taking part in the march through Deal when the Freedom of the Borough was granted to the Royal Marines Feb. 1945.

Robinson L/W Froud L/W Reynolds Milne L/ W Ollivant Keith Fletcher Hone L/W Hellyer Conroy
Garrad Winfield Townsend L/W Hall Webb Morrison Jones Bingham L/W Thompson McDowall
Hayes Dow Hart Falkinder Bradley Bordon McPherson Reeves L/W Hancock Kirton L/W Hough
James Guildford Goodwin Monaghan Waite Boys Williams Stock L/W Wyatt Wyer

P.O. Wren Dowson   H/NNA Whittle
C/Wren Hoy C/Wren Parsons 2/O. P. White, WRNS Col F. N. Grant 3/O. N. Chadwick, WRNS C/Wren Hansford C/Wren Hannibal-Williams

Left to right - Jane Wilson, Lynn Greem, Pip Tonkin, Anita Walton, Jenny Smissen, Marion Howard, Jane Gollop.

Mrs Thatcher visits the Royal Marines School of Music in 1983.

The Depôt Band 1890-1930

Formed in March 1890 the Depôt Band was a late-comer in joining the Divisional Bands of Chatham, Plymouth, Portsmouth and the separate Royal Marine Artillery Band. By recruiting from other Service bands, frequently the Army, or from civilian life, the Depôt Band's strength grew from 17 in 1891 to 32 musicians by 1902. The band's duties were to provide music for Pass Out Parades, Church Parades, ceremonial and social events in the Depôt or out in the local community.

A Victorian Bandmaster would have led a band consisting of piccolo/flute, oboe, E flat clarinet, B flat clarinet, bassoon, French horns, cornets, trombones, baritone, euphonium, bombardons and drums.

There were not many highlights for the Depôt Band in its brief life. It was disbanded in 1930 when the R.N. School of Music moved to Deal. However memorable moments were taking part in the coronation procession of Edward VII in 1902; playing for the Prince of Wales in 1909 when he dined at the Officers' Mess and accompanying the Prince of Wales in H.M.S. *Repulse* for the Royal Tour of West African colonies, South Africa and South America in 1925.

Two outstanding Directors of Music served with the Depôt Band. In August 1923 Lt B. Walton O'Donnell, with most of the musicians of the disbanded Portsmouth Division Band, arrived in Deal. This band had ceased to exist after the amalgamation of the R.M.L.I. with the R.M.A. in 1923. The distinctive helmet badge of the Portsmouth Division Band featuring the Prince of Wales Plume, was transferred to the Depôt Band, now renamed the Band of the Depôt, Royal Marines. Lt O'Donnell was one of three distinguished brothers who were also Directors of Music in Royal Marines bands. B. Walton O'Donnell was a distinguished conductor, composer and teacher. He elevated the band at Deal, now 35 strong, to its highest standard particularly by developing an orchestra. In 1924 O'Donnell left for the appointment of Professor of Military Music at the Royal Academy of Music, London.

When O'Donnell retired in 1927 he was replaced by Lt Frederick J. Ricketts, also known as the composer Kenneth Alford. Ricketts had served with the 2nd Argyll and Sutherland Highlanders for nineteen years. He only served at Deal for three years but his fame as a composer was established in his next appointment with the Plymouth Division Band.

The Depôt Band was formed in 1890 but it only existed for forty years before it was replaced by Royal Naval School of Music.

Church Parade 1911.

A Church Parade with the Bandmaster (left) marching alongside the band as he plays the French Horn, c.1912.

The Depôt Band Trooping on Church Parade c.1922.

An inspection of the Depôt Band in front of the Officers' Mess 1905.

The Royal Naval School Of Music 1930-50

The R.N.S.M. was founded in 1903 at Eastney to provide Royal Marines bands for ships of the Royal Navy. On 1 October 1930 the School moved into East Barracks, Deal. About 250 officers and men were led by the Band of the Depôt from the railway station, through the bunting-lined streets of Deal, into the barracks. The School quickly settled in and by 1932 they were supplying musicians for 40 ships' bands.

The 1930s was a difficult time with an economic depression nationally that was reflected in the Royal Navy. Recruiting was very difficult because of the unpopularity of continuous sea service expected of bandsmen. As a consequence an increasing number of boys were enlisted. In 1937 there were 360 band boys undergoing training at the School of Music, alongside 260 adult other band ranks. A boy joined at fourteen years of age and went to sea aged sixteen years. Life was hard for a boy but with talent they could go on to a great life and career. A role model was Lt Arthur Pragnell who became the Musical Director of the R.N.S.M. in 1935. Pragnell was the first Band Boy to become head of the Royal Marines Band Service. His Assistant Musical Director was Lt A.C. Green who, as Fleet Bandmaster, composed the setting of the bugle call 'Sunset', later to become famous when bands Beat Retreat.

The R.N. School of Music faced great demands for bandsmen once the Second World War started. Not only was the School to supply drafts to ships in the fleets but now there were many more ships coming from the Reserve Fleet. In addition there were the naval depôts and an increase in new training establishments requiring a band. At first ex-Royal Marines bandsmen, both non-pensioners and pensioners, returned to Deal. These pensioner bands were used for home naval establishments with HMS *Royal Arthur* (formerly Butlins at Skegness) being the first to have such a band. However the demand for bands was outstripping supply, so in the spring of 1940 'Hostilities Only' musicians were allowed to enlist. These men were professional and skilled amateur musicians in civilian life.

Recruit musician Joffre Swales in his autobiography *We Blew and they were Shattered* described what was to be expected of bands on sea service.

> Later in the day were summoned before a kindly Royal Marine Colonel for briefing. He told us that we were the third squad of raw recruits to appear before him. Then he continued, 'You have elected to serve in a world famous corps with great traditions, and we shall expect you to make every effort to maintain our reputation. You are about to start a course of hard military training with a view to making you obey orders without question. A certain amount of time will be spent in music practice and instruction, and playing in ensembles. After your training you will be drafted into a ship's Royal Marine Band which can range in number between twelve and fifteen. However, if a ship carries an admiral the band will then be increased by a further two musicians, for he has the luxury of an oboeist and a bassoonist. You are here today because we are currently experiencing a shortage of musicians on account of the commissioning of new ships, that is, cruisers, battleships and aircraft carriers. While your ship is lying in harbour, the band will be employed for ceremonial duties. They will also double as an orchestra for wardroom dinners, and a dance band will be formed to entertain the ship's company and help keep up their morale. But at sea, your action station will be the gunnery nerve centre known as the Transmitting Station, and situated in the very bottom of the ship. There you will be positioned around a large table with glass top, below which will be many moving needles, and diagrams of your own and the "enemy" ship. When the enemy is sighted all visible and available

information will be passed down to you from up top. You will plot these messages, sometimes known as "guff" into the clock, including your own and the enemy's speed, ranges, changes of direction relating to both ships, ballistics of the day, etc. The whole of this information is then electrically transmitted to the guns, thus giving them the necessary inclination. The ship's main armament will consist of four turrets, A, B, X and Y, X turret being completely manned by Royal Marines, both the turret and magazine. Each turret contains two guns, and in a "tell-tale" panel you will see eight dials, each of which will be illuminated when the applicable gun is ready to fire. You must bear in mind that your work at the plotting table will be vital during an action, because accuracy is the keynote, and an error could even result in the destruction of your ship. Your action station will be difficult both of access and exit, and it will be completely sealed off while you are at sea. It is situated between an oil fuel compartment and a magazine. Should a mine, torpedo or shell strike in your vicinity, there will probably be an outbreak of fire and it will be necessary to flood a number of compartments, including your own. But you will have to remain at your stations. The guns will need information from the plotting table until the very last moment. I have given you this factual information because a number of you will certainly lose your lives during the conflict at sea. In face, the Band Service has already suffered a number of casualties, and so I am giving all of you the opportunity of withdrawing from any commitment if you so wish, and you can continue your lives in civilian street.

The Royal Marines Band Service suffered profoundly in the Second World War with 225 killed, the highest percentage casualty rate of any service.

On 30 May 1940 the R.N.S.M. was evacuated from Deal. The 300 Band Boys went with Lt A.C. Green to the Royal Marines Reserve Depôt, Exton in Devon. A week later the 450 adult band ranks at Deal went to Stonehouse Barracks, Plymouth. However Plymouth was not safe or suitable, so in September 1940 both disparate parts of the School were moved to Malvern. They were split apart again in 1941 when the Boys went to the Isle of Man and the Seniors went to Scarborough.

The R.N.S.M. did return to Deal but it was to be in momentous circumstances. The wartime, itinerant School had one more move, to Burford in Oxfordshire in 1946. In 1948 the training of Boy Buglers was transferred from the three Royal Marines Divisions to the R.N.S.M.

The wind of change now swept through the Royal Marines and particularly the Band Service. Disbandments or cutbacks were the harsh options of the day. The Corps was scaled down, Chatham Barracks were closed but these compromises meant the Corps survived. The Band Service, it was noticed, had two distinct band branches involving duplication and weaknesses.

The R.N.S.M. trained boys from the age of fourteen, formed bands and drafted them to ships and shore establishments. A musician could be sent to any band at home or abroad, ashore or afloat. On the other hand the Divisional Bands enlisted trained musicians and they remained in the same band throughout their service. As a result they were good musical teams with a higher musical standard. The bands provided by the R.N.S.M. served in ships for the length of its commission (about $2^{1}/_{2}$ years), and then they were broken up and re-formed for other ships and shore establishments. It was not possible to achieve such a high standard of teamwork. Also, a ship's band had to be small because of a lack of space in a ship.

In 1948 the Leech Porter Committee recommended the amalgamation of the three Divisional Bands with the R.N.S.M. to create a unified Band Service. The plan was implemented by the new Commandant General Lt Gen. Sir Leslie Hollis in 1949. When the R.N.S.M. returned to Deal its fate was already sealed. The Boys' Wing returned in January 1950 closely followed by the Seniors. In February 1950 a staff band was created for the R.N.S.M.. The amalgamation took effect on 1 September 1950 with the headquarters of the new Band Service in Deal at the re-designated Royal Marines School of Music.

Tennis courts for the Royal Naval School of Music in East Barracks, 1939.

The Royal Naval School of Music moved to Deal from Eastney in 1930. This is the Salon Orchestra for the Officers' Mess with Lt A. Pragnell c. 1932.

On an impressive but unknown stage this is the R.N.S.M. Band in 1935.

Forsdick Williams Brooks Elston Hough Boden Stenning

Beardmore Allen Dyer Beardsall Bowbrick Rumney Riley

White-Sanson Pether Tompkins Booth Badder Cox Griffin Pearce (SC) Ayling Wastall

*B.E.M. Q.M.S. Jackson, L.R.A.M. Q.M.S. Catchpole C.S.M. Wells, B.E.M. Q.M.S.S. Breeze, L.R.A.M. C/Sgt Rendles Sgt Jones (Instructor)
Cpl Nevitt B.M. Reynolds, Cpl Skinner*

*Lt K.A. McLean, L.R.A.M. Col P.R. Smith-Hill, C.B.E. Lt Gen Sir Leslie Hollis, K.B.E., C.B. Major M. Pound Lt Wm. Lang, L.R.A.M.
Lt G.C. Perkins Lt J.H. Blood*

(Musical Director) (Commandant RNSM) (CGRM) (OC Boys Wing) (Asst Mus Director)

(2 i/c Boys Wing) (adjutant)

The Royal Marines School Of Music

A snapshot of the year 1950:

The total number of Royal Marines Bands were 34, varying in strength from 15 to 28 musicians. With over 1000 in the Band Service, about half were at the School of Music.

The Boy Musicians received general schooling as well as musical training. This was particularly important following raising of the school leaving age to fifteen in the 1944 Education Act. So those joining at fourteen years had to receive a similar education to those in secondary modern schools. The boys were organised into 'Houses' each named after one of the ships in which Royal Marines Band ranks lost their lives in the Second World War. They studied the usual main subjects in well equipped classrooms, including drama and handicrafts. This was all a far cry from the pre-war R.N.S.M.

The boys' accommodation was in East Barracks while the S.N.C.Os and trained musicians lived in modernised blocks in North Barracks or flats in married square. The training facilities included the continued use of the old chapel in Canada Road as a concert hall. The old attached school rooms became the Theory Rooms. The Musical Workshop was in a large hut between the barrack block and Royal Buildings.

Boy Musicians drew 10/6d (52p) a week on joining, 14/- (70p) after one year's service and £1.8s.0d (£1.40) on reaching the age of seventeen and a half years. At eighteen years they became Musician 2nd Class on £1.15s.0d. (£1.75p) a week; a Musician 1st Class drew £2.5s.6d (£2.27p). A Band Sergeant aged thirty, married and with three Good Conduct Badges earned £7 per week. Accommodation, food, clothing and heating were supplied free to the single men.

1951–1996:

The 1950s was a contrasting decade of contraction of the Band Service yet there were major innovations and growth at the School of Music. The number of bands declined from 36 (in 1950), to 31 (1952) to 21 (1959) of which only six were serving permanently afloat. In 1957 the Macmillan Government imposed severe cuts on the Royal Navy and Royal Marines. In two years the Band Service fell from 1000 all ranks (1958) to 800 (1960) including 16 officers.

Back at Deal, the appointment of Major (later Colonel) F.V. Dunn as Director of Music, quickly elevated to Principal Director of Music, transformed the work and quality of musicianship of the School of Music. In the winter of 1954 an annual series of orchestral concerts began which aimed at expanding the orchestral conducting experience of Bandmasters under training at the School. These concerts also introduced internationally famous conductors and soloists to appreciative audiences who went regularly to the Canada Road concert hall. Colonel Dunn's advanced training policy led in 1955 to two Bandmasters being sent to the one-year conducting course at the Royal Academy of Music. The success of this initiative established the course as a regular feature for all subsequent Bandmasters and Band Officers.

By 1958 the benefit of a unified Band Service, the Royal Marines School of Music and Colonel Dunn's training standards were showing a dividend. There was a recording contract for the School of Music Staff Band and the first 'Beating Retreat' on Horse Guards Parade in celebration of Prince Philip's birthday. In 1964 the largest massed bands ever, over 380 musicians and buglers, performed the ceremony of Beating Retreat, Horse Guards Parade. Earlier this huge body of musicians had rehearsed at Deal. In January 1965 the R.N.S.M. and Portsmouth Bands took part in Churchill's funeral procession.

On 10 October 1968 Major P.Neville took over as Principal Director of Music when Lt Col Dunn left the Corps after thirty-eight years of distinguished service. The new era did not open well with the announcement of defence cuts calling for a reduction in the Band Service strength from 750 all ranks to 500 by 1973. By late 1981 the R.M.S.M. was the sole occupant of the Royal Marines, Deal. However, the contraction did not seem to diminish the demand or workload of the R.M.S.M. Band. Under the leadership of Lt Colonels Neville, Mason, Hoskins and Ware the standards of the School and its Staff Band continued to go from strength to strength maintaining its unrivalled position.

Behind the polished public performances was the necessary support from Headquarters. At the R.M.S.M. was the Director of Music Higher Training, who conducted all musical promotion courses in the Theory Rooms together with a civilian Professor of Harmony and R.M.B. instructional staff; the Director of Music Junior Training responsible for the selection and training of all junior musicians on their two years two terms training cycle in East Barracks, aided by his 14 civilian tutors and 20 R.M.B. instructors; and the Supply Officer (Music) who supervised the complete supply of instruments and sheet music not only for the Royal Marines Band Service, but also 20 R.N. Bands, together with repair facilities for musical instruments, the drum repair workshop, and the Central Music Library used by all Royal Marines and Royal Navy Bands. Assisting the P.D.M. was the Assistant Director of Music who managed the day to day administration of the Staff Band.

The future of the R.M.S.M. at Deal never seemed to be off the agenda from the 1970s. In December 1976 the Government announced that proposals were being considered to close the Depôt and move the R.M.S.M. to Eastney. By 1980 the Government made a further announcement that the Eastney option was delayed.

In 1984 the Government White Paper 'The Central Organisation for Defence', set up a consultation period for a new Defence School of Music at Deal with an intended completion date in 1988. In 1987 the plan was abandoned and Royal Marines, Deal was re-designated as the Royal Marines School of Music, Deal.

The final years of the Royal Marines presence in Deal began with a big chill. In January 1987 so much snow fell in Kent that Deal was cut off. The snow drifts on the approaching roads were up to 8 feet deep. Food ran low and as fuel supplies became critical, the heating was reduced in the offices and messes.

The sell-off and demolition of parts of Deal Barracks began in 1988. King Charles Court and the Infirmary Barracks were sold for £1.2 million and £3 million respectively, the M.T. building and two of the old accommodation blocks were demolished.

On 22 September 1989 at 8.25a.m. tragedy struck the R.M.S.M. An I.R.A. bomb, placed in the Recreation Room of the North Barracks, exploded. Some of the Staff Band was relaxing prior to a rehearsal for a ceremonial event in Strasbourg the following week. Only 200 yards away, the Junior Band were rehearsing on the main parade ground. They were the first rescuers at the scene. Ten musicians were killed that morning and another died of wounds a month later. Three civilians were also killed. The School, the town, the nation were shocked, angered and saddened.

Those who died were:

Musician M.L.P. Ball	Musician C.R. Nolan
Musician J.A. Cleatheroe	Band Corporal D.P. Pavey
Band Corporal T.J.E. Davis	Musician M.T. Petch
Musician R.G. Fice	Musician T.J. Reeves
Musician R.M. Jones	Musician R.L. Simmonds
Band Corporal D. McMillan	

A week after the atrocity the whole R.M.S.M. with W.R.N.S. and Naval Nursing Staff, marched through the streets of Deal with a depleted band. Poignantly there were spaces left amongst the ranks of the marching band. The P.D.M., Lt Col John Ware was defiant in his determination that the band would carry on playing. A memorial service was held on 22 November in Canterbury Cathedral.

A landmark event in the history of the Royal Marines Band Service occurred on 1 September 1992. The first ten female Musicians began their training at the R.M.S.M.

The Royal Marines School of Music finally closed in March 1996. The final parade was by the R.M.S.M. and other massed bands on 22 March 1996.

Drum Major F. Tobin leads the Boys Band, 1952.

H.M. Queen Elizabeth The Queen Mother at the opening of New Accommodation Block, North Barracks, 23 May 1956 with Col. B. Lumsden Commanding Officer. This block became the most superior quality accommodation in the whole Corps.

The spanking new Accommodation Block.

The Block contained 96 eight-man dormitories for other ranks, 12 single rooms for S.N.C.Os, modern furnishings, hot air central heating and 68 roses in the forecourt garden.

Musician Kevin Vickers receiving cello instruction from Inst. Lt Harrison. 1959.

Capt. E. Ough conducting the Boys Orchestra at Deal, 1954.

On completion of training a Boy Musician is examined by Capt. McLean, Director of Music in 1952. Also in the picture are Capt. A. Talling and in the back row Staff Bandmaster Bone, B/Sgt Jennings and B/Sgt Shilletto.

Promotion students for Musician to Band Corporal attending a Music Appreciation Lesson with Lt Topley R.N. 1952.

A section of the Boy Musicians Symphony Orchestra being conducted by Lt 'Pop' Talling, 1952.

M.J. Styles, H.T. Busby, S.J. Cowling, P.F. Nunn, N.F. Henshaw, S.S. Ascott
D.J. Pennington, I.D. McLean, S.P. Hallam, B.K. Jones, G.W.F. Bingham, A.T. Burgess, D.M. Williams
C/Sgt Scott, S/B.M. W.C. Greasley, R.L. Alberry, A.J. Osborne, J.R. Malpass, Bug. Maj. J.W. Wagstaffe, C/Sgt R. Thatcher
Lt Cdr K.J.B. Topley, Major C.E. Boothby, Lt Col Vivian Dunn C.V.O. F.R.A.M., Lt E.S. Ough L.R.A.M., Lt A.J. Donald

(S.I.O.)   (O.C. Boys Wing)   (Principal D. of M.R.M.)   (D. of M. Boys Wing)   (Squad Officer)

The Junior Dance Band 1959.

The Junior Band in East Barracks canteen, 1959.

Capt. T. Ough conducts a concert orchestra, 1959.

The welfare role of the Church at the Royal Marines School of Music had a high profile in the 1950s, as this publicity photo and articles in the Blue Band *magazine demonstrated.*

The embarkation band for H.M.S. Lion *getting some final rehearsals in with Bandmaster P. Toms, 1962.*

Smith, B. Baker Thomas, R.S. Simmonds Symington McRoy Willis Elcock Bridgland Deacon Hayward, E.C. Pugh

Blandford Mann Bradshaw Wood MacKay Smith, R.J. Paige Bennett, A. Clarke Shaw Swann Wilson

S/B/M W.G. Greasley, C.S.M. Sgt A. McVicar, P.T.I. Sgt R. McCubbin (Squad Instructor) Bug. Maj J. Wagstaffe (Bugle Major)

Thomas, F.L. Piner Aves Williams Darley Bennett, R.T. Hayward, C.J. Nicholls Pike Carter Fulton McCurdy

Lt W.J. Mansell, M.C.   Inst. Lt-Cdr K.S.B. Topley   Maj L.H.D. McCleod   Col B.J.D. Lumsden, O.B.E.   Lt E. S. Ough   Lt A.J. Donald

(Adjutant)   (S.I.O.)   (O.C. Boys' Wing)   (Commandant R.M.S.M.)   (Dir. of Music)   (Squad Officer)

Drum Major Tobin, a survivor of H.M.S. Barham, *with Peter Hughes, cornet player and Gordon Twine with the bassoon, 1952.*

The R.M.S.M. Staff Band leading the Guard of Honour for the Captain General through Queen's Street, Deal, November 1957. The Drum Major is Charles Bowden with the Director of Music 'Pop' Talling.

Lt Col V. Dunn instructing a Bandmasters' Class 1959. Apparently a posed photo because the frock coat would be overdressed for a normal occasion.

Can you name all the faces at Bandmaster Owen Williams' 1960 party to recognise twenty-five years' service?

John Maddy pushing dents out of the bell in the Instrument Repair Shop 1962.

The same repair shop but in 1977 with Musn J. Guest and Mr R. Charters.

Rehearsal for the Massed Bands, Beating Retreat, Horse Guards in 1960.

The same 1960 rehearsal. Capt. 'Dizzie' Lang faces the bands in his characteristic pose.

The Junior Wing Band and Junior Marines, North Barracks 1964.

Lt Col Paul Neville succeeded Sir Vivian Dunn as the Principal Director of Music in 1968.

Professor Mike Thatcher M.B.E.

Professor Frank Boyden.

Bandmaster David Wells.

Bugler/Drummers under instruction from Bug. Cpl McCartney.

The I.R.A. bomb atrocity 22 September 1989.

The victims were having a coffee before going onto the Parade Ground for rehearsals.

In memory.

The Memorial Bandstand opened in 1993.

A public relations photo to record the first women to join the Royal Marines Band Service, 1992.

The first women under training must have felt great pressures by being the forerunners of a new era.

Infirmary Barracks sold for £3 million in 1988.

The demolishers moved into the barracks in 1988. The Infirmary Barracks were demolished to make way for housing.

The Infirmary Barracks on their way to being converted into Bamford Way. Built in 1909 these barracks once housed a large part of 41 Commando.

King Charles Court sold for £1.2 million in 1988.

The converted East Barracks in the year 2000 with its new residents.

North Barracks awaiting demolition, 2000.

The one-time Gymnasium is eerily quiet. Even the ropes and wall bars remain in place with echoes of past days.

The Royal Marines last parade through Deal, March 1996. The salute was taken by Brigadier R. Tailyour R.M. and Mrs Eileen Rowbottom.

Lieutenant Colonel Sir Vivian Dunn, K.C.V.O., O.B.E., F.R.A.M.

In the long illustrious history of the Corps Lt Col Sir Vivian Dunn remains one of its most distinguished figures. With a career of thirty-eight years in the Royal Marines, including fifteen years as the Principal Director of Music at Deal, he greatly elevated the status and standards of the Royal Marines Band Service.

Colonel Dunn was born in Jubbulpore in India, the elder son of Captain W.J. Dunn, M.V.O., M.C., Director of Music, Royal Horse Guards, who at the time was Bandmaster of the 2nd Battalion, The King's Royal Rifle Corps (60th Rifles). His mother was also a fine musician so that the young Vivian grew up in a musical household.

His education followed strictly classical lines via the Konservatorium de Musik in Cologne, the Royal Academy of Music, where he came under the influence of Sir Henry Wood, and the Queen's Hall orchestra. As a violinist and junior conductor this period of six years was one of intensive musical study. He became one of the original members of the first violins of the BBC Symphony Orchestra under Sir Adrian Boult in 1930. In 1931 at the age of twenty-two Vivian Dunn applied for and was accepted for, the post of Director of Music Royal Marines (Portsmouth Division) against strong opposition as this was a unique appointment direct from civilian life at such a young age.

For the next twenty-two years Lt Dunn led the Portsmouth Band at Eastney. By 1953 he had established an elevated and influential position. He was appointed to the newly created post of Principal Director of Music for the amalgamated Royal Marines Band Service with the rank of Lieutenant Colonel. At Deal, in the new R.M.S.M., he had the challenging task of bringing the Royal Naval School of Music musicians up to his high standards. Many of the old school musicians were resentful of the amalgamation and the radical changes. Colonel Dunn set about his task by focusing on training and the provision of new instruments, thus ensuring a raising of musical standards. Although the fruits of this work would take some time to be noticed, it did establish the quality of Band Service renowned from the late 1950s onwards. It was his idea that aspiring Directors of Music attended the Royal Academy of Music for a year's attachment, a perception that was to pay dividends.

During his career Colonel Dunn had the unique privilege of serving the Royal Family in the reigns of King George V, King Edward VII, King George VI and Queen Elizabeth II in the Royal Yacht and on Royal Tours to South Africa in 1947 and the Commonwealth in 1953-54.

Col Dunn directed the Massed Bands of the Royal Marines on numerous occasions when Beating Retreat for H.R.H. The Prince Philip's birthday, at the Royal Tournament and the Edinburgh Military Tattoo. All these televised events made Sir Vivian a well known figure to the general public. He also became universally known through recordings of 78s, L.P.s and E.P.s and spanning a period of 28 years, culminating with the award of an E.M.I. Golden Disc. He was also a prolific composer and arranger. *Cockleshell Heroes, The Captain General, Soldiers of the Sea, The Admiral's Regiment, The Globe and Laurel* and the *Preobrajensky March*, and Mountbatten Suite to name a few. A full list of his compositions, arrangements and recordings is included in his biography 'Fiddler on the March' by Derek Oakley.

When Col Dunn retired in 1968 he became the only military musician ever to be knighted and left a legacy of a Royal Marines Band Service in a supreme position of quality and musicianship. The Royal Marines School of Music became renowned as a centre of excellence which has continued to the present day.

Vivian Dunn joined the Royal Marines in 1931 as Director of Music, Portsmouth Division at the exceptionally young age of twenty-two years. In 1953 he was promoted Lieutenant Colonel and made Principal Director of Music at the re-organised Royal Marines School of Music, Deal.

Basil Kidd

Lt Col Dunn was a renowned composer and arranger. Here he is handing the score of his new W.R.N.S. March to the Director of W.R.N.S. Commandant Dame Elizabeth Hoyer-Millar. Also in the picture are Capt. T. Parker R.M. Staff Officer and Second Officer Craig-McFeeley, O.C.W.R.N.S., Deal. October 1960.

Lt Col Dunn towards the end of his distinguished career which had lasted thirty-eight years. In 1968 Lt Col Dunn was honoured with a knighthood for his outstanding service.

Corps Drum Major Charles Bowden
B.E.M.

Charles Bowden served twenty-two years two months as the Drum Major of the Royal Marines School of Music, Deal. However, Charles Bowden's outstanding career with the Royal Marines began long before this memorable era.

Charles came from a family with a distinguished record of service in the Royal Marines, both grandfathers, father and three uncles and a brother having served. In 1923, at the age of seven, he joined the Royal Marines Cadet Corps at Eastney Barracks, Portsmouth, wearing the old Royal Marine Artillery cap badge and becoming the Cadet Sgt Major. He joined the Royal Marines in 1940 and became a sergeant within three months. He soon found himself in the Near East with the 1st Mobile Naval Base Defence Organisation, involved in the Battle of Crete. Charles was taken prisoner by German parachutists whilst in hospital but he escaped in his pyjamas, boots and cap and rejoined his unit. He was involved in bitter fighting in a rearguard action against heavy odds. When the day was lost, a party of 138, under Major Ralph Garrett R.M., embarked in a damaged landing craft to make their escape. After nine days at sea on an almost non-existent diet of corned beef, biscuit and water, landfall was made in North Africa, near Sidi Barrani, where Sgt., Bowden carried out a recce, located a British unit and then led his companions to safety. Service continued in the Mediterranean until late 1943, when he returned to Britain to train troops for D-Day, he himself serving in France from July 1944.

After Victory he served as a Military Training Instructor at the Depôt, Deal, taking the King's Squad to the Royal Tournament in 1947.

He became Drum Major in 1950. From then on he went from strength to strength leading the Staff Band at no less than 12 Royal Tournaments, 5 Beat Retreats on Horse Guards Parade , 6 Edinburgh Tattoos, the 1953 Coronation, in addition to becoming a well know figure in all parts of the country on band engagements. He accompanied the Band's visit to Vancouver in 1958, Toronto in 1959, to the United States and Canada in a long tour of 1965 and at the Sierra Leone Independence ceremony in 1961.

Drum Major Bowden was presented to the Queen Mother in 1956. He was awarded the British Empire Medal in 1957 and presented to the Queen at the 1971 Royal Tournament. Charles retired in 1972.

Drum Major Charles H. Bowden B.E.M., R.M., served the Royal Marines School of Music as a Drum Major for twenty-two years two months, the longest period known for any Drum Major in any Service. Charles Bowden's total Royal Marines' career lasted thirty-two years three months.

Drum Major C. Bowden leading the R.M.S.M. Band for the Royal Tour in HMS Vanguard *in 1952. Regrettably King George VI died before the tour started.*

Subscribers

Lawrence Abbess, Kensington

Richard J. Ablett, Deal

John Stuart Ainley, Deal

Alfred J. Allen, Essex

Jim Allen, Chipping Campden, Glos.

Susan P. Allen, Emsworth

John Ambler, IMMS - UK Chairman

Albert Archer

Maurice and Elizabeth Ascott, Deal

Lt Col Jack Ashman, RMR Tyne

CHX 4293 A. Atkins, 45 Comm.

Thelma C. Aubourg, Deal

Arthur E. Awcock, Canvey Island, Essex

Roger Stephen Baggs, Deal

Robert David Baker, Deal

Roy D. Ballantyne, Canterbury

Sheila Bamford, Isle of Thanet

Pamela Bancroft, Dover

Godfrey W.B. Barnett, Deal

John Barnett R.M. Ret'd, Droitwich Spa, Worcs.

John D. Barrett, Deal, Kent

Mr James Bassett BEM, Tyne and Wear

Mr J. J. Battershall, Essex

Major Peter Baxter, Deal

Joan Bay, Broadstairs

Robert G. S. Beaden, Deal

G. Bealby (ex Cpl.), 45 Commando. Beckenham, Kent

C. G. Bean, Colchester

W.B. Bell, Hull, E. Yorks.

Harold B. Berry FRTPI, Liskeard, Cornwall

Tom Bevan, Eltham

Les Biggs, Falkland Islands

Michael John Billett RM., 996 Squad. Ipswich

Nigel Bogue

Chris Bogue

Mr E. A. Bond, Gillingham

Mr Tony Bond, Deal

Ian (Sticks) Booth,

Kenneth Booth, Worcester

J. M. Bouch, Peterborough

Mr and Mrs C. H. Bowden, Porlock, Somerset

Colin E. Bowden, Malvern, Worcs.

Margaret A. Bowden, Deal

Colonel Gerry Brace (Retd.), Bristol

Roy V. Brittain, Birmingham

Ron Broadley

Alfred E. Brown, Cambridge

John (Buster) Brown B.E.M., Gateshead

Fergus J. M. Brown WS., Peebles

William J. Bryan, Deal, Kent

W.O.D. Buchanan, RM Corps Drum Major 77/81

Jim Buchanan, Kent

Major K.A. Buckingham, RM

Eric G. "John" Bull

D. J. Burch, Golden Cross, Hailsham

Mr Keith Burden, Kent

Marine (D) Ian Campbell, RM 19191 Southsea

D. M. Campbell, Stornoway

Mr and Mrs A. Capper

Little N. Carlisle

Sam Carragher, RM 7865   528 Squad

Jack Carter, Chesterfield, Derbyshire

Colonel B. L. Carter OBE, Alverstoke

Ex WO2(D) I. Chapman, Norway

Lt Col. M. J. P. Chilcott

Chis Chisling, Crawley

Paul A. Clark, Poole

Cyril Le Clercq, RM 7535. Deal, Kent

Joan P. and Edgar G. Cole, Whitstable, Kent

Jean Coles-Walker

Ken Collingwood, Salisbury

Cpl R. Collins, RM 16132 Croydon

R. Collins, SGT RMR RET, Hampshire

Carol Ann Conway, Deal

Mr R. A. Cooper, Deal, Kent

Martin "Coopes" Cooper, Peterborough

Roger Copelin, Brighton

"Sticks" Cordery, Plymouth

Corps Historical Records Officer

J. B. Corrigan BEM

Ex Marine Ch/X 114291 M. H. Couchman

Jock Cowan, 588 Squad Oct. 1951

Robin C Cowling, Kent. RMB 3046

Stuart Cox, Deal

L. W. Cozens, Deal, Kent

Mrs Moira Crook, Deal

Eileen Crow, Deal, Kent

(Ex) PO20493K C/Sgt J. Cruickshank

Ronald Curry, Newcastle

Clifford J. Daff, Spalding

Martin and Heather Dale, Deal

Mrs Pauline I. Davison

Vic Day, Ex RM 11380 Shrivenham

J. Dick, Portsmouth

Major A. J. Donald RM, Horndean

Captain P. G. Downs, RM. Ret'd

Sylvia Dunford, Dover

Mr Ian Durban, Southend-On-Sea

Alastair Eager, Worthing, Sussex

BCSgt Ray Edwards, Yeovil, Somerset

Mrs Sheila Eldridge, Deal, Kent

Dennis A. Emerton, Australia

Dennis "Lofty" Emerton, Floraville, NSW, Australia

Kevin England DC., Croydon, Surrey

Les Evans, Deal

Robert Evans, Dover

Mr and Mrs G. F. Everitt, Deal

Mr Robin M. Evernden, Kent

Cpl. C. F. W. Fairey, Plymouth

John Farlie, Potters Bar

Rocky Farnworth

Brian C. Fawcett, Walmer

Henry (Harry) Femister, Edinburgh

K. G. Fields

Eileen D. Fillis, Walmer

Richard Michael Follett, Deal, Kent

William R. Foord, Sutton, Surrey

Peter J. Foot, Bedhampton

MNE (Del) Ford, Welling, Kent

Desmond J. Forwood, New Ash Green, Kent

Sgt Vince Francis, USA 908-707-8111

Paul N. Franklin, Deal

Mr Michael C. (Tex) Freeborn

G. M. Fryer, Felixstowe

Lt Gen Sir Martin Garrod, KCB CMG OBE DL, Deal

A/Ty Lt A. H. Gibson, Exeter

WO2. Bandmaster. G.R. Gill, 4.1.55. - 27.4.80.

Jack Goddard, London SW2

Captain A.M.W. Goddard, RM Ret'd

Marine (Titch) Golder, Lowestoft

Captain Paul Goodlet RM., Chard, Somerset

George Gotts, R.M.

Roland J. Graham, Carlisle, Cumbria

John Graham, Lochgelly, Fife

Eric J. Green, Eltham

Harold E. Greenhalgh, Ferndown

N. Griffin (Griff), Birmingham

The Griggs Family, Deal

Major (SCC) C. Guiver RMR

Mr Ron Haggis, Battersea, London

Arthur L. Hammond, Plymouth

Ernest E. Hannabuss, Kent

J. W. (Tosh) Harding, Chatham

Mike E. Harris, 19477 772 Squad

Geoffrey Richard Hart, North Cheam

William G. Haston, Deal

J. A. Hatch, WO2 Ret'd Malvern Wells

Professor Martin Hattersley, Chichester

Major A. J. Hawley RM., Curry Rivel

Graham Hayes, RM. Mucn.

Mr C. Hayes

Former RM Wren Joan Hayward, Deal

William B. Heal, Deal

Kathy and Ray Heine, Walmer

Ernest Hemmings, Shropshire

Mr J. F. Hetherington

Mr William Hickey, Chartham

Major P. J. Higginson, 756 Squad, 1961

Stan Hocking, Manchester

Lynda M. Hodgson, Deal

Captain E. J. Hogg, RM. Pettistree

Arthur J. Holmans, Faversham

Marion and Ivan Holness, Deal

Eric E. Hook, Yorks

D. A. Hope, RM 1947-49

Bill Hopkins, Sussex

Margaret G. Hopper, Kent

Mr W. Hoskins, Malvern, Worcs.

D. J. Hougham

Mrs E. Hougham, Deal

WOMA Phil Howes, DMSTC

Peter Howse, RMBx 2627 Gosport

Mr and Mrs R. V. Hubble, Deal

Tom Hurst, Prestolee

Michael G. Hutton, Newbury

Arthur Jackson, Reading

Marine E. H. Jackson, California

Mrs Patricia Jakes, Kettering

Kenneth C. Jamieson, East Sussex

George L. Jarman, Eastry

Captain B.A. Jeffs, RM. Plymtree

Harold "Jimmy" Jimmick, London N8 0HT

Denis A. Jones, Buxton

John R. Jones, RM 7797 Southend on Sea

Musician Mark Lea Jones, Dalgety Bay, Fife

Ron Jordan, Marlow, Bucks.

Mr A. R. Jordan, Deal

P. W. Josiah, Morden, Surrey

Brian E. Joyles

T. A. Judge B.E.M., Cheshire

John A. Kelly, Deal

Richy Kenderdine, N. Yorkshire

A. Joe Kendrick, Deal

Revd F. Kent, Ex Bandsmaster

Len C. Kerr, Former R.M.

D. C. Kevill, Deal, Kent

James R. King, Crawley

Rip Kirby, RM17395, 695 Squad. Hull

Geoff Kitchen, Essex

Frank Knowles, Knutsford

John Kruthoffer, Leeds

Gordon E. Lambourn, Ripley, Derbyshire

Terry J. Lane, Torpoint

Geoffrey J. Law, St Albans

G. T. Lawrence, Canvey Island

Reginald A. Leach, Kent

David John Lee, Fair Oak, Hants.

Kenneth R. J. Legg, Swanage

Captain R. J. Leigh, RM (R'td)

Ex CSgt "Lynx" Lincoln, Plymouth

Meg Linggood, Mallorca

Peter (Nipper) Lockhart, Lymington, Hants.

Edward Lovell, West Sussex

WOII(YofS) Tony Luckman RM. 775 Squad 1962,
41 Cdo RM 1982

POX 5910 QMS Terry Lyndon, Portsmouth

Robert Mackintosh, Plymtree, Devon

Ron Maggs, Southborough, Kent

J. Maitland-Ward

Ivan Marsh, Wingham

Clifford Marshall (Plymouth Division), Verwood, Dorset

William Martin, Carlisle, Cumbria

Stan Mason, (PO/X 5099) Exeter

Mrs Valerie P. Maxwell, Deal

Walter W. McCrae, Kilmarnock

Rodney McCubbin, Ex QMS/First Drill RM

Mr Finlay McCulloch, Corsham, Wilts.

James R. McIlhatton, Stranraer

Bill McKenna, Cheshire

Captain Jack McNulty, Kingsdown

Horace E. Mendham, Deal

Colin Mier, Chatham Marine Cadets

E. C. Miller, Brighton

Michael Mizen, Norwich

Mr Cliff Moiser

Mr Kevin A. Morris, Marton, Cleveland

Ray Mosley, 6th May 1959 - 2nd August 1962

F. W. Mottram, Durham. 615, 1953

Col. Sgt. J.A.B. Munton, Plymouth

Ronald Musto, Hainault

Mrs Joy Newman, Chipping Norton, Oxfordshire

John (Nutty) Newnham, Shrewsbury

H. Newton, Worsley

Ruth Nicol, St Margarets, Nr Dover

Bob Niddrie, Morestead

Frederic E. Nolan, Plymouth

Rory O'Callaghan, Weymouth

Sean O'Callaghan, Deal, Kent

CPO (SCC) M. O'Keefe

Michael O'Sullivan

Peter Osborne, Chatham Ex RM

Denis Ovendon, Former Royal Marine Bandsman

Mick Page, Perth, Western Australia

Mrs M. E. Palmer

"Sticks" Palmer, Hatfield

Peter G. Parsons, Kent

Peter M. Pavey, Eastbourne

Philip H. Payne, Bishops Lydeard

Mne R. Pearce, 87 Troop Aug '73-Jan '74. 41
Cdo RM '77-'78

Donald Peart, Darlington

Mrs Pat Penn

Roy M. Pepper, Adelaide

Bryan J. Percival, Alderley Edge

Charles E. Perkins, Eastry, Deal

Polly Perkins (Sigs), Exmouth, Devon

Mavis and John Philpott, Canterbury, Kent

Mike Pinchen, Chislehurst, Kent

Plaisters' Company

Qms J. A. Porter, RM, Ret'd. Deal

David Powell, Captain RM. 1936-1946

Douglas W. J. Powell

Mr W. Power, London

George Pray, Toronto, Ontario, Canada

Mr Harry W. Prescott, Deal

Rodney Preston, Portsmouth, Hants.

Wilfred Price, Cheshire

Mrs Hilda Price and Family

J. C. Puddle, Deal

Mr D. L. Pugh, Manchester

Mr A. J. Pugh, PLYX 5485 Birmingham

Peter Quill, Essex

L. I. (Tod) Raven-Hill MBE., Twickenham, Middlesex

Peter L. Rawll, Glos.

Bernard G. Rawson, Cambridgeshire. 924 HO Squad

Capt F. W. Rayers, (Ret'd) Malvern

C/Sgt (SCC) A. J. Read

Vic N. Redsull, Bath

Geoffrey Richards, Hilperton

Mr and Mrs D. Richards, Deal

P. J. Roberts, Deal 1969

WO2 Al Roberts R.M., Ivybridge, Devon

H. A. Rogers, Welwyn Garden City

John Rogers, Deal

Michael Rogers, Faversham

POX 112050 Marine Don Rogers, Stafford

Major D. M. J. Rogerson, RM

John Roke, Gunners Row, Southsea

William Ross, Edinburgh

Commandant General Royal Marines

Royal Marines Corps Secretary, Portsmouth

Mrs Ailsa Rushbrooke, Essex

Marc Russell, Broadstairs, Kent

John "Fritz" Salzmann, Aldermaston

Andrew Sargent, Deal, Kent

Takashi Sasaki, Japan

John Satchwell, Carlingford, NSW, Australia

E. H. Schofield

D. J. Scott, MNE. 128777 NS

Jackie Semple, Northern Ireland

Wilfred (Brummy) Severn

P.C. Shapter, 977 Squad, Plymouth, Devon

Irene E. Shaw, Deal, Kent

Sidney George Sheard, Deal

S. G. Sheppard, Spalding

Mrs J. M. Sherratt,

Ann Shields (nee Walker)

Colonel R.C. Sidwell OBE, Sidmouth, Devon

Evan Simpson, Chester le Street, Co Durham

Ken Sinclair (Cpl), 713 Squad Jan 1959

Daphne M. Skinner, Deal, Kent

S.E. Skippings MBE, Recruit 1940 Po/4829

J. Smee, RM. 8633. 541 Squad 1948

Bryan R. Smith

Mike Smith, 42

Ken Smith XRM, Canada

Gordon E. Snowball, Lancaster

Michael George Sole, R.M.B.

David P. Stennett, Deal

Mr Geoffrey Stevenson, Deal

Major General P. T. Stevenson

Dr J. Bernard Stillwell, Lethbridge, Canada

John R. Stoker, Deal

Bernard Stonestreet, St Leonards on Sea

Reg Sully B.E.M., At Deal January - September 1936

Joffre Swales MBE, Haverfordwest

J. P. Synnott

Mark Talbot, Watford

Brian N. Tarpey, RM14099, Sliema, Malta

Eileen Taylor, Folkestone

R.O.K. (Rocky) Tebble, Ealing, nee Croydon

Patricia E. Thomas, Luton, Beds.

Ex Marine P. A. Thompson, Long Melford, Suffolk

L. J. Thomsett, Deal

A. H. (Tiny) Tinham, Chatham

Robert Todd ("Geordie"), RM 10135, 45 Commando,
                                                    Deal

Peter D. A. Toms

Ethel M. Tonkiss, Kingskerswell

Douglas C. Trotter, Doncaster

G. H. Turner LGSM, RM Band Service

Richard Valentine, ex RMB 4069 1965-1976

Marine Alan Waite, HMS New Foundland Assco.

WOII (D) Ron Walkerdine (Ret'd), Spalding

James Walter, PO/X 116816. Seaford

Geoff Walton, Deal

Bill Ward, RM 17620. Deal, Kent

G. Wardhaugh, Ex 520

Major E.H. Warren MBE. RM., Dorchester

RM Fred Waters, Herne Bay

Ray Watts, Wiltshire

Paul Watts, Exmouth

Mr R. F. West, Ex 3127

Ken Whiterod, HMS Anson Association

Major J. Whitty MBE RM

Allan Wilby, Plymouth

Christopher Wilkinson, Peel, Isle of Man

Terry Williams, Deal

Lt Col Philip A. Wilson, RM

Ross M. A. Wilson F.C.M.H., Ottawa, Canada

Sylvia Wiltshire (nee Reeday), Deal

L. G. J. Woodhall, Caersws

Mrs Joyce Woods, Deal

Peter Worsfold, Deal

E.A. Wright, PO/X 6181, Isleworth, Middlesex

Peter L. E. Wye, Ply/x117156 (976 Squad) Clacton-on-Sea, Essex

Derek Yardley Wright, Stonehouse, Glos.